POSTCARDS FROM LOS ANGELES

NICK MARCOTTE

Postcards from Los Angeles

by

Nick Marcotte

ISBN: 9781694822963
Imprint: Independently published

Dedicated to Nathan Temple

Let's catch an air show sometime.

My Friend,

Congratulations on the arrival of your first child. I couldn't be more overjoyed at the news—and that everything went well. I appreciate all your updates, and have certainly been thinking about you.

I'm also reaching out because, although It's taken me awhile, I feel it's time to share with you the pages that follow.

These postcards speak of a time and a place—when I lived in Los Angeles for a season of my life. They mean nothing, yet they mean everything to me. I don't have much to offer the world, but perhaps I can say something true—or what seemed true at the time. This little collection is a compression of experience, of about three years or so. Each of these poems a minor psychological event, where I felt I should record the weather patterns inside.

Remember when I left Austin? That late 2014 time?

I remember a lot of darkness then—and I'm not trying to be dramatic or literary in saying that. I quite literally remember the darkness—nighttime at your place in East Austin, under those orange alleyway streetlights. Pulling up to your place in the gravel, after work. You took me in, and I'll always be grateful that you did. It was around Halloween. That penetrating dark, nights spent having homebrews with you, the glow of the T.V. You never asked me any questions or accosted me for any of my reckless decisions. You were just a friend.

A few weeks later I was in L.A., driving in on the 134—backed up in traffic in the dark. My first taste of that L.A. traffic I'd always heard about. I was thinking about Texas and that last Texas sunset I saw—idyllic and complete with the oil drills. Cormac McCarthy on audio.

You were with me the entire trip. I had a broken heart like a country song cliché, and some part of me was damn proud of it. I knew it wasn't a mistake to try and love—in fact, it was one of the most worthy things to try for. And this would become clear to me in the years that followed in Los Angeles, perhaps as these poems reveal.

What else can I say, my friend? Here is a little log of one life, in one time, in one place—a very big place, and a very little life.

My corner was called Glendale, but I explored a lot beyond that. I returned to my teenage home of San Diego, and even went up as far as Santa Cruz for a wedding. L.A. was nothing like I had imagined, which is perhaps the most obvious thing anyone could say.

Then again, there were moments when something came together—the sunshine on the mountains off the back patio, Jackson Browne's first album on the record player, my brother in plain sight right next to me, young and alive and drinking coffee, as we talked about things to come. Dreaming collectively as Angelenos like to do.

I don't know if I was ever an Angeleno, but I felt like one for a while. I had always wanted to be one, at least since I was a teenager—and was mystified by Jackson Browne, the Eagles, and all the movie stars and luminaries of old that once occupied the city right up the road from me. It seemed so simple and within reach to me as a kid in San Diego.

I'm glad that L.A. is where it is, and that I'm in Albuquerque now. This transient life has been hard on the heart, yet one of my greatest gifts. Every place I've ever lived still lives within me.

My favorite moments have been the quietest ones; or ones where I looked at someone I love when they weren't watching.

I want you to know I love everyone and everything here—even, and perhaps especially, the moments of dissonance that come through.

Don't ask me why I feel compelled to share them—that remains a mystery to me. But I will admit that I hope these provide some kind of roadmap through suffering—or at least company, when none can be found. There is just as much joy here as pain, and perhaps even more joy.

I'm certainly grateful for the experiences that led to these writings—and please don't think that they are all actual. Some are just expressions of the life of the mind.

I love you, my friend. I always will. I hope these postcards will keep you company—wherever I am, and wherever you are.

Nick, May 2019

CONTENTS

IV. Childhood

V. First Summer in Albuquerque

VI. Postscript

The Hardest Part

The hardest part of being an artist
in my opinion
is that it sometimes involves
making yourself naked.

But if you can be comfortable
walking your naked body
down Highland in Hollywood
you can do just about anything.

I.

First Winter in L.A.

Take Me Back to Austin

A lot of my dreams take me back to Austin—
the crowded bars
the dinners with friends
the people I never met but did

The way the city changed with the weather
the Central Texas gloom
moving, shimmering
with cars and more condos

Hurts my head to think of
having one more PBR on East 6th—
drinking from the heavy metal
one more before last call
besides girls with boyfriends in bands
and tattoos on their legs.

We find some queso & chips somewhere
(there's plenty around here)

Fat and salt melt in the boiler room of my belly
filling me with Texas comfort
just beneath the plaid and pearl snaps
that I can't seem to suck in enough,
but let me tell you:

The best cure for a heartbreak is a food truck.

That's where she left mine—somewhere in the dirt nearby
beneath an airstream
after a self-conscious meeting
with friends
at a bar

where we were poised to take on our careers
and she said,
"I'm too smart for this shit"
unwilling to do anything about it.

We had big hearts and big egos—
but our egos we kept hidden,
shrouded in the blankets of
false gratitude and good times.

Dolly Parton

I remember we watched that thing on Dolly Parton—and I was moved to tears by how much she loved Porter Wagoner.

And I looked outside, to the hills beyond your apartment, and thought that there was a whole other way to be.

We ate our low-fat ice cream from the freezer and thought about Monday. These things always in our minds:

> -our bank accounts
>
> -my pending move
>
> -is the dog okay?
>
> -what's for dinner?
>
> -how long will it be until we're naked again?

and for me, country music. And a song I couldn't tell you about.

I would sing anyways.

In the shower, while you got ready by the sink.

I spoke the words to an old song to you as we lay in your bed one afternoon. You may have been asleep.

I hoped they'd reach your heart somehow.

Like somehow you would get to know me if I spoke those words clearly.

And you would know what kind of man I am.

A bond would form that could never be broken,

and I would be connected to you always.

I Kissed You on a Thursday

Our lives were kept in the sun
like kids by poolside
in a summer of learning to swim.

The heat cooked the concrete
and we walked quickly to not get burned.

Our hair getting bleached
our legs dangling in
never worrying about
the imaginary sharks.

I kissed you on a Thursday
we hoped no one could see
and I knew I was in it.

Tell me one summer that was ever risk-free
insurance purchased in advance
just a phone call or two
and you'll be safe for the summer months
(said no one ever)

But at least we had sushi
and I put my arm around you as we left the restaurant

it was the first time I had felt someone in a long time.

The Art of the Reasonable Chance

Days are spent in parking lots

You have to cross them
no matter where you're going.

And I count this time with letters to a friend
handwritten
some typed
each symbol forming a skin
around meaning

Some meanings reside on the upper shelf
just a jar full of colors that I keep reaching for
others are here already
rainy days
and a beautiful face in the car

my beautiful friends who sit somewhere out of reach
their lives drops of color in that jar
I sometimes draw them out
drop them onto a page
and watch them spider out;
these brief moments I had with them.

I'm much more reasonable now.

I go to the post office.
I help a lady put postage on a package
going to Issaquah, Washington.
It has hearts on it
It's Valentine's Day
and I imagine the person receiving it
is a soldier.

The day begins to rust,
and there's only so much time in a weekend.

I buy a new pair of athletic shorts
I fix the car
I take my brother and his girlfriend to the airport
I daydream about punks.

I am practical, I am impractical
I am the shark, I am the flower
I am the sugar in my veins
I am a new pair of shoes
I am a night out in Hollywood with no money.

I am the taxes that need to be done
and the bills that have already been paid
I am a phone call to a friend
even when I don't have time.

I walk the sidewalk from the post office
and try to correct my posture.

I have not yet mastered the art of the reasonable chance.

Valentine

I have seen
evenings by waterside
the sun shining
through her eyes
and told her "I love you"
without words

Here on her patio
she is someone
I've always known

We're students
of these fields
as we look beyond
the house

Examining each other
in the quiet
of our hearts,
her eyes
meeting mine

Silent questions
turn to night
as she gives me
blueberry wine

I'm sleepy
as the album repeats
for the third time

It may be
that she hopes

to keep me
and this time
I oblige

But we do not kiss
and we do not touch

as we search
each other
for love.

Hit Send

Packages arrive

the hours just slide

and she's been on my mind

I type a message

in a Facebook box

these space-age names

connecting us by a thread

Hit send

and send again

I wait in the sun

away from everyone

waiting for someone

to pass the time with

No More Waiting

your car rolls down an L.A. street
collecting the sun's glare

you never thought 33 would be like this
(those are miles per hour not age, by the way)
and there's no more waiting today

There's no more waiting for the sun's flare
or for the light to go green
you never thought 33 would be like this
(those are miles per hour not age, by the way)

There's a place in the city you want to drive down to
a sign that glows at night
there's people all over this city
making things alright

and there's no more waiting;
this is everything you need.

There's no more waiting at age 33.

Katherine

The last time I saw you, I knew you were a poet.

The way you commanded the calm,
and drank wine into your last days—Corbett Canyon
("taking a walk in the canyon," you'd call it).

We lost you in the Winter of Skepticism—
the winter I lost my belief.
I had just moved to L.A.,
and heard about your death
in the parking lot of a bar.

On a phone, I could barely hear—
because there were young men laughing nearby,
in the prime of their lives,
young women too,
out on a Thursday night.

They told me you wrote into your last days,
and there were projects undone.
My brother and I looked at each other and said,
"let's not leave any projects undone."
And the night went on.

Then I stayed in the space you stayed in
just before you died.
It was filled with your books and affects;
your mind spread throughout the room.

I looked through it.
I found a letter from your husband, and read it—
and then apologized to you,
telling you I was only looking for direction.

I wonder if you heard me

My life was no different at first—
Jimmy Buffett playing in the garage,
as we threw a frisbee in the street.

Then someone presented an article about you
from when you were 26,
working as a tour guide at the United Nations.
You were working on a book at the time—
about what, I can't remember.

I think it was about the place you came from;
the plains of Colorado.
You were writing about the people there
that came before you and worked.

You worked—
        in the library you worked,
        in the quiet you worked.
Work is what you knew.

You parted from us in Albuquerque in 2014.
I wonder if you ever saw yourself there.
In that room, full of books.
Letters that somehow stayed over the years.

They weren't mine to read, but I was lost.

So I went looking for letters.

And I found you.

II.

The Softening

Garden

Where is the girl
who's as bright as the sun
as pretty as the moon
and wants to share a garden with me?

We would cross the street
in Santa Barbara
looking both ways twice.

Our love would feel
like it feels
to walk inside on a summer day,
your eyes adjusting.

And as the sun sinks low
the garden would be shadowed
which is the perfect time to walk in it.

The Softening

she took me by the hand
back when they still did that
back when our faces were young
and we looked like play things.

the morning in her face
a morning for me to see
though I may sleep
here is my awakening:

"age is a dimming of vision"
a friend of mine says to me.
the world doesn't sully,
we simply see less.

so what a gift now
to see you like this

because now I see all creatures differently—
this heat doesn't bother me.
I soften my tone when I speak to my friends
in gratitude of the blossoming,
and the way you took my hand.

you took me by the hand
back when you still did that
back when our faces were young
and we looked like play things.

Muted

I can feel love in the muted sounds of this town

in the echoes of the cars going by

in the cantinas down the street

in every glass of beer

in the flies that land in my ear

I can feel memory speaking back

finally

whispering details

facts mostly

like the day you and I spent going to the garbage dump

and how it came to be

one of my best memories of you

How our brotherhood

was finalized that day

and how that time still lives in my heart

like a silly metaphor

"two friends in a pile of trash"

nothing seems more real than that.

—San Diego, 2015. For John.

Hills

Do these hills talk back?

Did they memorize the times we were here?

Do they reminisce the way that we do?

How do they feel about the sun falling each day?

And what do they do in the rain?

I can't seem to find her name anywhere around here

I want to ask the hills if they remember her

and see if our memories match

Because she was a sight to see

a beauty

and I wonder if these hills

ever looked on with envy.

—*San Diego, 2015.*

Valor

Tell me of your valor

of the battles you fought

of the love you lost

of the way you walked by the sea

and the way you loved perpetually

Tell me of the places you lived

of what you killed

and what you lost

and how you moved through these canyons

to eventually come back home.

Put your fire into words

let them burn on a hill for all to see

put them into freckled skin

that I want to kiss

Tell me of the storms that came

how they changed the color of the frame

and did you remain

elegant?

Did you stand your ground during difficult times?

To which you reply,

"I know nothing

am nothing

but what I love

and who I love."

—*San Diego, 2015.*

Dinner in Alpine

The sun,
a canticle of remembrance,
allows this one visit:
        The whine of the truck in 5th gear
        a Mitsubishi motor
        and the first time you heard
        Jackson Browne on tape
        the Interstate 8
        heading east toward Alpine
        your father there
        the sun giving light
        to what would stay forever in your mind:
        the perforated upholstery
        under teenage fingers
        a dream, a song from another time
        a head, still taking shape
        a body, barely begun to bloom
        and the nobs on the radio
        playing the "Cocaine" blues

        the sun said goodbye
        and you learned to love the night
        as you finally arrived
        for dinner in Alpine.

Jackson Browne

My favorite photo of you

is the one where you're at the piano

face untouched by time

looking outward

toward the window

your back to the shadow

hands on the keys

building songs

of your generation

the photo sings

as clearly as you do;

Henry Diltz there that day

with camera in hand

Was it just the two of you?

And where did you go afterwards?

Maybe into L.A. for some tacos?

Maybe for a joint on the patio?

Where the summer sun

shone in full resolution

the details of the canyon

the heart of the city at a distance

yet also, within you

What did you think about there in your collared shirt?

Where did your thoughts travel to?

and how did they appear

when they returned

ready to be married

in a secret wedding

to music?

When night falls on sorrow

it is never in vain now—

thanks to the songs you wrote.

Sage of The Quiet Song,

tell me what it was like to be you—

to discover your youth in L.A. in the streetlamps

to walk in with your guitar

at the Rouge et Noir

to examine the distance

and the inner sanctums

of the heart

Now it may be

that the hardest thing I've ever done

was to write some words about you—

but words are what you gave me

They dropped

into the suggestion box

of a teenage boy in the 1990s—

who carried it around

the halls of his high school

mixed in with the words

of a great teacher

and a few good friends

with whom

he would sometimes share

the words of Jackson Browne.

And for me,

the evening will always belong to you—

even as I become The Pretender

with little to show but some words

and some money I made

and the belief that the world

can be made better for our children,

even as we fade.

Nate

I close the blinds on a Sunday night
and think about
how now you're gone.

Planes pass by outside
like they did in our youth
at this time.

I close the blinds on a Sunday night
ready for bed—
this could be 1998
but it's 2016.

The air feels the same
as it always did
at this time—
still, and pregnant
with the week.

What will be born this week?

Will I give what I've always given?

What will die this week?

Will someone lose a friend?

I lost you on a day like any other.

I remember the last Facebook comment you left me;
it was about *The Karate Kid*.

Those are the kinds of things we talked about—

the 80s still lived within us.

I listened to 80s music endlessly
the summer that you died—
creating a space around me;
a synth-pop dream in 2015.

I can't listen to 80s music now.
Not for awhile, anyway.

The plane sounds have died down,
and now there's a helicopter circling.

I thought maybe
I'd see an airshow with you
in San Diego,
where we used to live
when we were kids.

But that plan
got eaten up
by the months
by nights like this
of closing the blinds
and airplanes outside,
and pregnant weeks
that promise something.

They always promise something.

But the truth is
lives go by
in these evenings of nothing.
In the hum outside of

distant flying things.

Reminding us that we can always take flight.

III.

Coffee & Donuts

July 3rd

We celebrate in the shadow of an aircraft carrier.

Our fried food;
oiled fingertips with salt
it's satisfying.
I drink a Lite beer
way more than I need.

"The sauce is good," says the man next to me.

And I feel the grease on my chin before the sun sets.

Fish & chips
a portrait of Americana
with my hair did
a cheap wrist watch
a shirt that's buttoned up with short sleeves.

"That was better than I thought," he concedes.

My eyes move up
passed the boardwalk and the battleship
(the harbor's full of them).
I know a lady in the Navy
but she's not here today.
It's just me.

The breeze fills sails as motorboats go by
under the watch of war machines.

I see myself as a Navy man
some portrait of Americana—
a life I've never had.

And everyone seems to have a dog—
which is as American as anything.

The Padres lost today.
San Diego seems frustrated.
People search their phones.

I see an old Mariners hat. I like that.
I used to live near Seattle.
I like seeing Mariners hats down here, by the bay.

The sun lights the last of the day
and we see the silhouettes of fighter planes.
I feel safe among them.
I feel pride arise—
critical, though I am, of my country.

"Do you know how much I ate?" Says the man next to me.

He's cleared his plate
calzone and all
spent packages of parmesan
his lover to his right.

How lucky we are.

A man's pulled his hat over his face
sleeping precariously on the sea wall
the edge of the boardwalk
his Nike socks pulled up.

I'm him.
My grateful lethargy rests on this bench.
I contribute to the economy
I pay my taxes
I vote (though I missed the primary).

These American modalities.

I am grateful for my set of problems.
I do not ignore the crying of my country
the unutterable sorrows I cannot recount
(they are countless).
I do not have the diagnosis.
I do not have the remedy.
I want her healing.

I finish my beer and see the sunset
through the base of a plastic cup;
way more than I need.

The dogs fight
and I think of my country.

Girls walk by
and I think of my country.

I cannot see the sun behind the clouds now;
the sun I came to see.

And I think of my country.

Spanish

Thank you for Spanish

I love this language

I love to hear it

(even though I understand 15% of it)

They speak it next to me

It feels like a painting

Copy vs. Poetry

I'm a dried-up rat who doesn't wanna come back from vacation.

I spent the weekend writing poetry
now I'm writing copy again.

It takes some time to change languages
and they don't always understand each other—
like estranged siblings who grew up to be different.

This one's the businessman, this one's the artist.

Though they live in the same city
and go to the same cafés
they date different women:
the women who date Copy
have no patience for Poetry
(Poetry's aims seem fruitless and vague).

Poetry has fewer dating options, but good ones—
and those women don't really trust Copy, as they shouldn't
(Copy's always selling something).

Poetry can't really seem to get his shit together,
but he *is* sincere.

They're brothers with different color hair
who secretly want what the other has—
and maybe that's why they don't get along.

They usually speak at holidays, but only briefly—
one giving up his place for the other.

Both are languages of novelty and sensation

of arousal of desire.

One makes false promises and the other doesn't.

I started the weekend with Copy
and ended it with Poetry.

I miss Poetry.

Old Glory

No need to polish old glory, my friend
not with the life you've lived

Just put pen to paper
and see what comes up

Because there's a reservoir of truth
that lives beneath your days—
you can go there anytime
and draw from it something fine

When you put words to music
the finest silk comes out of your mouth
your voice soothes me
and calls lovers down
and takes me back to those Berkeley afternoons
of open windows and jazz
and how the light
fell just right
on that building downtown

We wrote about that kind of thing—
and you lived to sing about it

You tossed that old vase water out the window
and it nearly fell on Fancy Dan—
we laughed until our nostrils flared
and got high with the magpie

Those were good days.

Then someone took the life out of you—
you found yourself on your back

on a street
in a different downtown
San Diego
when that guy mistook you for someone else
and punched you so hard it took your music out
your throat closed shortly after that
a cist, you said;
the night your music went to bed

Now you sit in quiet contemplation
the sun falling on your golden hair
like a king among his riches
who has lost his sight
and is unable to recognize them.

You take the guitar out of the case
from time to time
and text me a recording you made
on a Sunday
like the Sundays we passed in Berkeley
when sadness would win the day

Feel free to send me your songs—
they'll be my lullaby.

And should you ever regain your sight
you will see
that you are a king among riches
drawn from the inside.

The gold within you
comes out of your mouth—
pour it onto the floor
and watch it fill the boards
of all the places we've lived
and you will have the songs to sing

No need to polish old glory, my friend
not with the life you've been given.

For Z.

Let Me Be an Artist

Let me be an artist
let me be under your boot
I will walk the streets of Paris alone
trying not to be a cliché
that will be my business
as you go about yours

But if you have a minute
let me show you this poem I wrote
(the gray skies will make the paper especially bright)

You'll see my brow furrow
as I try to read to you
in a voice that is my own.

Let that be my business
I will write about yours

I will write about the way you hold your coffee cup
and the ring on your middle finger
I will be happy when the rain starts to fall at this café
and I have to put the damp pages away

Let me be an artist
as we part ways
and I leave you to the life
you think is worth pursuing
and you leave me to mine.

Most Things Are Coffee & Donuts

—the most mundane reception

no one will ask your age
no one will be rude

and if they are, it'll happen under fluorescent lights
while everyone drinks mediocre coffee
from mediocre cups
that will end up in a Saran trash can,
someone undoubtedly tossing theirs away
before it's finished.

and that person will seem unpleasant
and out of place
and you'll just look at them

They'll be the crazy one in the room
not you.

Then the book signing will resume
or the meet and greet
or church
or lessons
or whatever

the author's hair is thinning as he signs books—
no one cares

people drink crappy coffee from crappy cups—
no one cares

They're just glad to have coffee.

They're thinking of the next thing to get to.

They're hoping that their own hair isn't thinning.

Because most things are coffee & donuts—
a quiet shuffle in the morning
half asleep
with hope for pleasantness
and a hope for the taste
of something sweet.

The Default Religion

Is being young and marketable.

But what happens when you're not as young and not as marketable?

I look around my life—
        into my past
        into my future
        anywhere but here

I even become religious again for a time.

Anything to not bow down to the clear-cutting—
to the mechanical behemoth that moves through our homes
our bedrooms, our workplaces
making everything the same

neutering souls

pacifying youth culture

all while convincing us that this is an event worth attending.

It is not about "anymore" or "we used to"

It's about the flatlining of pulses
        removing the untamed edges of things
        a wild haircut working an office job
        about two or three candidates
        and deciding
        based upon who is the better fighter.

There is no room for expression anymore

it is contained to a computer screen
Self-Expression Privatized.®

I'm seeking only the sullied ends of the earth.

More Than Pleasure; A Love You Can Rely On

I can sing songs for you at the end of the day

I can hold the door for you

and ask

if you like Old World romantic gestures

I have good style

you will always look good standing next to me

I can help you with your finances

I am a nerd

I can help you balance your budget

at least in basic terms.

And if you were to lay across a bed

with the evening sun coming in

a part of me would fall down

and never get up again.

But all of that's to say

how would you like to end the day?

Because someday soon there will be dust on our couch

and a cat so fluffy and gray

he doesn't seem to care that we age.

And we'll find ourselves in blankets

with tired eyes and hair.

And you'll find that you have a love that you can rely on.

Santa Cruz

Lay light blue tissue paper over the sun
and you've got the coast of Santa Cruz

Smile goofy with your headphones on
and you've got me

See salted bodies in the surf
and you've got the beach

Here we are
at the edge of where we came from.

I Listen for the Wind

I listen for the wind to call my name—
to take me through the streets of Glendale
over deserts and back to Texas.

My windows rolled down
I like to feel free
even in my own neighborhood.

The Verdugo mountains are quiet tonight
even though I know the wind is there—
coming down with new intention
or intention that was always here.

I move around
to San Diego and back.
In the dusted windshield
I see the sun focus its energy.

I listen for the wind to call my name—
to tell me where to go
if I should remain
or go back to places I've been
in some new skin.

IV.

Childhood

Rubber Sharks

I remember your tears
as we sat there
in a Rax
shortly after you left dad
on a porch
in Columbus, Ohio.

We didn't understand then
but we knew how to cry with you.

Then sometime on the road
there was cereal from a box
Fruity Pebbles
as you struggled to see through the rain.

"Slow down!" And you said his name.

Tears again
and then we were in a motel room
where I played with my rubber sharks
on the bed.

Oceans for covers that stretched for miles
while someone had the gall
to watch Playboy on the television,
thinking we were asleep.

Back on the road until we found ourselves
in Seattle
the ice relentless
the late 80s
gray and faded skies
water streaking the window.

I first saw my cousin on the porch
the welcoming committee
dancing
looking much happier than dad looked.

Ghostbusters in a basement somewhere
cousins crying.
We began our life in Monroe
now living with your sister.

I looked forward to those fast food nights
at a park, on the swings, under the orange.

The windows rolled down at night
where the wind ripped into me
and the darkness crept in
along with the smell of springtime
and the sight of foliage in the headlights
driving to our apartment in the country.

That place that was just above the farm
where we kept ducks in the house
and they shit everywhere
but we loved it
and we loved them
as you sat alone in the darkness
with no light but the receiver
listening to "Nothing Compares 2 U"
or Peter Gabriel
or something else
I can't remember.

Slurpees

Cigarettes & sunshine
cancer slowly cooked
in the backseat of a Thunderbird
the seats slightly torn

the red leather
cheap by today's standards

the hood
lightly brushed in dust
burned my hand to the touch

the silt
from the ashes of a fire
last winter

abuse
covered in sunglasses
the tears shed
and cooled
by something from 7-11

it felt good to put a Slurpee to your skin
after getting yelled at
or spanked

we were just the children of our parents
and they the children of theirs

who never intended any harm.

Spanaway

Pretty sure she knew the words to every Boyz II Men song.

That's what we heard on the bus
on the way to school
in the snow.

Desire born inside
as I rode in silence
eyes on the icy waste
dead grasses reaching out
bushes pushed down
like frustrated spiders.

When I got to school it was far from "I'll Make Love to You"—
puberty wasn't for another year or two.
And my generic bomber jacket
didn't have the logo
to get me the status I wanted.

Shorts worn beneath the jacket
my socks pulled up to my knees
with a Nike swoosh—
at least I had *that* going for me.

Hair frozen to my head with gel
and too much Suave—
it was the best chance I had.

K-Mart cologne in my pocket
stolen from a locker
by another kid who gave it to me—
I'm ready to be popular.

Don't read fantasy novels in study hall
it doesn't build you up at all
but that didn't stop me—
Marcus freestyled a song
while I thumbed along
and read about a red mage.

I should do the homework
I didn't do the night before
but it's probably too late now anyway.

He got beat up in the boy's bathroom—
an initiation—
but when his friend who brought him
saw what was happening
he turned against the gang
and defended him.

I didn't see the brawl
just the kids gathered in the hall
and then the bell.

It was dangerous to be seen
so we wore all the clothes we could
and only dreamed
of taking them off for anyone.

Leanne and Leejay
and all the names that start with "L."
My boy was Deejay
and we spoke that slang;
the language of the radio.

We lived our lives
watching the corners
and over our shoulders

on the way to 7-11.

Everywhere we went
a vicious attack—
if not on your body
then on your mind.

You were dead at school
if you crossed the wrong guy.

Was it really all that?

Hormones and dreams
have a way of bending the light
when you wake up on a couch
on a Saturday
after a night of seeing aliens.

Until the world is restored
if only for a weekend.

I Dreamed of a Mountain

I dreamed of a mountain
that washed away my past

It took away the feeling
and gave me what was left

I dreamed of a mountain
that brought me to the morning

Even as it lay
in the orange blanket of evening

I grew up near a mountain
in the Pacific Northwest

I could see it from where I stood
on the playground, in the cul-de-sac

God gave me a mountain
to live inside my mind

And when I lose my way
I can see it anytime.

The Citadel

As we approached the citadel,
it reminded me of something I had seen in
fantasy art from the 90s:
        a black mass beneath hovering spires
        winged beasts, barely discernible, circling it
        a hellish scene.

        And on the plains below, the heroes—
        fleeing as though pursued
        or something was about to blow
        while the ominous castle looked on
        with dark indifference
        its sheer surface polished, impenetrable
        who knows what dwells there
        (I always wondered)
        and what those heroes were after
        and perhaps didn't get
        were they making an exit with the treasure?
        or had they been turned away by the terror?
        I always thought that they had gone
        and got what they needed inside
        and that the deed was done;
        that the danger was behind them now.

Now we are in that scene
and the citadel is before you and me
it is where we must go
because it is yours

I see the fear in your eyes, my friend
they are sunken in
and I see the age
and how long you've carried this

I am here at your side
with my symbols and light
we are not children anymore
though that's when we met
and now, as men, we will go in

I will locate the entrance if you cannot
and we will take the head
of the thing that haunts you

I don't claim to never be afraid—
but I am brave when it comes to you

I will fight along your side
and I will face the darkness
that has draped over your life.

And the moment will come
when we enter the chamber
in the heart of the tower
and you will see your foe

Then I will hold it in place
so you can look in its face
and see what's plagued you

And you will feel pity
as tears stream from its eyes
over its charred skin
and you will see it's none other than
Hurt himself
once the lord of this ruined castle
now nothing more than surrendered deformity
asking to be freed

And you will release him
bloodlessly
as your fear dissipates
and you will roam these lands
once again
which are
and have always been
rightfully yours.

Space Needle

I can't tell you the relief I felt, standing in line to go up into the Space Needle.

"Life is happening here," I said. And I felt the gloves on my hands, the nip of the cold air, the candy cane in my mouth.

And I felt at that moment that I could say anything, that I could pour out over Seattle, and I'd be okay.

Life is not happening through the abstraction of screen, is it?

Our faces were only lit up for a few moments by our phones tonight, but mostly by the lights within, and by each other.

My phone eventually died—that tail that connects me to the world abstract. A portal into my fears that are faceless. I try to impress the faceless audience always, constantly hoping that she's watching, or that he's not—all the while there's this towering artifice above me, built in a time of no phones.

Not the kind that trail us anyway.

And for me, art is just something that I love, an act of desperation saying, "I am here." Or, "life is happening now."

I don't understand the known world, but I'm learning it's not as mystical as we think. This structure was built with human hands for a World's Fair.

I tell the girl in the elevator I thought things built for fairs weren't meant to last. This was different though; this was meant to be here a long time.

And when we see the city, it's a manmade quilt. I wanted to catch my brother and his girlfriend just right in the photo, so you could see the eons stretching out before them.

—Seattle, 2014.

V.

First Summer in Albuquerque

Concussion

It wasn't so much that it hurt—
just that he put up a wall in front of me
and I was in the middle of it.

I spent the following week in a fog.
And one night the child in me cried,
"I don't wanna get hit in the head."

Consciousness swings
like a pendulum
between bewilderment
and clarity.

One moment I was driving
in the white light of an overcast day
Mother's Day cards stacked and stamped
in the passenger seat

the next I looked on in confusion at the calendar
as I was sure that meeting was today
and not the day after.

What day is it?

I didn't tell anyone but my brother at first, who said,
"if you've lasted this long, you'll be fine—
your body is already doing its work to repair."

I didn't do any heavy lifting
as he moved the last of his things out that night.

The blood thins as it moves through that region—

I press my head hard and feel some relief.

Somewhere inside there's a nick in the gelatin—
like a Jell-O cake that's been picked at
at a depressing summer picnic.

One night I drive to 7-11
for some Tylenol and some cookies
the moon is almost full
and I take comfort in my short road trip.
And I think how if I left for Albuquerque now
I could be there the next day.

Then on the bed with Jackson Browne playing
on a speaker by my head—
I only give myself what I need when I'm hurt.

Fear subsides
and I get used to the cloudy water that persists.

Pressure contracts
and it feels like the shot landed somewhere in the center of my
head—
loosening the thoughts, the anger and the romance
that led me to want to box in the first place.

I think how now I'll double down on defense.
I won't get caught like that again
and I won't spar for awhile—
since one more of those might actually kill me.

Now out of the shower in a towel
in front of the mirror, doing a faux face-off—
a near middle-aged man
with something to prove to himself
maybe to others

maybe just to say:

"My shell is not as soft as it seems.
I can take your worst into my core.
I can be beaten, and still be here.
Every strike makes me more."

The Moon and I Leveled With Each Other

The moon and I leveled with each other

over the blood-stained desert

where the creases in the earth's skin catch the last light

The moon and I leveled with each other

on a plane, in discreet conversation

he told me why love is a great business

The moon and I leveled with each other

until the drinks came by and I passed

and the clouds came by

and made him play dress-up

in a white mustache

The moon and I leveled with each other

and I asked about his charm

and what it takes to stay so high

until it was time to land

and he said,

"It's just the way I am"

Bellies

I am very happy here now
in the sunlight
reading this book
on the floor
beside this dog
whose leg twitches slightly
as her brain shifts with dreams

on her face a serene smile
the kind only dogs can give
as the sun warms my back
my ashen skin

glad for the time
and the books
and the dog

as both of our bellies
rise and fall
in the dust.

Dreams Rise to Meet Me

The Albuquerque wind blows
outside my window
moving the dust in the yard
giving these curtains something to do

And I think about her
who I just met
and the Arizona sunset
and which desert I like better

Here I am
in a polished life
further refined by sand
and time
finding myself on airplanes
traveling one desert to another
as dreams rise to meet me.

VI.

Postscript

Receipt from L.A.

Damn
we had a lot of margaritas
at 13 bucks a pop
on Sunset Boulevard;
3 brothers tossed
more than 3 back

I must've paid
because I found the receipt:
       the margs number 7
       I had at least 3
       plus a Miller Lite
       and a chimichanga plate
       #15

That day we checked in on each other
as brothers should:
       you a cameraman now, recently engaged
       you an actor-to-be, still in the fitness scene
       and me a writer, maybe
       who recently moved away.

They brought us our check
and returned with the receipt
that says,
MICHELLE
"THANK YOU FOR VISITING"

We told our last jokes on the sidewalk;
where they were printed on the trash
that has since blown away

Until our cars arrived

and we parted ways—
beginning the ride home
to wherever that will be

on my breath a plea, as always,
to the city of Los Angeles:
"please take care of them for me"

Now, I throw the receipt away
and discard what is owed—
knowing that the sum
is always subtracted from
what we have saved in love

which is more than enough.

Acknowledgments

Thank you, reader, for your time and attention.

To all who have given feedback, love or support:
I send my love and thanks to you.

I'd like to say a special thank you to the following people for being among the first to hear and read these poems—and for their valuable feedback: Heather Calvillo, Lea Evangelista, Megan Frost, Lara Indrikovs, Sasha Lauren and Jackson Truax. Thank you all for making me and the work better.

Thank you to my brother Derek Lin for your friendship, support, our poetry nights and for sharing your work with me—and for inspiring me to take up the language of poetry when no other language seemed adequate.

Thank you to Lee Davis and Nathan Temple who have had a particular and special influence on me, and on this work. You both shined in life and continue to shine.

A special thanks to Derek Law who has been a true friend and encouragement since the night we met in Austin and bonded over Springsteen.

Thanks to Mike Karimi, Jennifer Na and Jennifer Yip for some insightful discussions about poetry. Also, thank you Jennifer Na for our poetry exchange—and for reading some early edits of some of these poems. I'm grateful for your feedback as well.

I'll always be grateful to the Ditzler, Frost, Law, Lin, Marcotte, Moghanian, Prebo, Sandlin, Temple, Walsh, Wu and Zubel families for their love and support through the years.

I wouldn't be who I am (and this work wouldn't be what it is) without my brothers Aaron Marcotte and Trevor Marcotte— I love you boys. Thank you both.

Thanks and love to my sis Delaney Moghanian for her support— and for giving me the opportunity to read some of these poems publicly for the first time.

I'd like to send my love and thanks to my parents Michael Marcotte, Valerie Marcotte and Denise Marcotte. It's safe to say none of this would be possible without you.

Thank you as well, Jasmine Lin and Jeremy Lin, for your constant love and support.

Special thanks to my brothers, "The Nicks"—Nick Temple and Nick Zubel. You boys mean the world to me.

Thank you, Mahdi Gad, for your guidance and friendship.

Thank you, John Ditzler, for more than I can say.

Thank you to my great friends since college, The Woolsey Men.

Thank you, Gabriela Gómez, for everything.

A special thanks for the support and friendship of Anthony Caruso, Nicole Garcia, Zac Garver, Rick Hawkins, Anna Mezhebovsky, Ka Young Park, Mikel Weigel and Debbie Yen.

Thank you as well, Shaun Pauling, for your friendship and mentorship.

Also, thank you Patrick Ojeda.

Thanks to Amanda Demock, Christian Glakas, Marco Gutierrez, Kirsten Longnecker, Cristina Madrigal, Martin Manuel, Emily McLeod, Dan Nettles, Amanda North, Carmen Ojeda, Skottie O'Mahony, Stephen Pfister, Cody Pruitt, Dani Pruitt, everyone at Kasasa, and all the other good people I know in Texas.

A big hug and thank you to Jack Canfield and everyone I've met through his events.

Thank you, Cassandra Rochelle Fetters, for pushing me passed the finish line—and for all of your encouragement.

I'm grateful for the places I've had the honor to live in and be inspired by; including parts of California, Georgia, New Mexico, Ohio, Texas and Washington.

Thank you Glendale and all of Los Angeles.
Some part of me will always dwell there.

Thank you Shiva, our pup, for being at my side on so many working days.

Thank you to the poets, songwriters and other artists whose work has influenced me, who are too many to name here. I hope to do for others, in some small measure,
what you have done for me.

Thank you to Amazon, Canva and everyone who made this publication (and printing) possible.

To all who have contributed to this work directly or indirectly:
thank you.

And though I do not have a clear spiritual concept at the time of this writing, I do thank God—or that which is the source of creation. I'm so grateful for all of this. Thank you.

Index of Titles

Made in the
USA
Columbia, SC